Vicki Howie writes stories, plays and songs for young children, based on her work with the age group in the local church. She is author of Barnabas' popular resource books Easy ways to Christmas plays, Easy ways to seasonal plays, Easy ways to seasonal fun for the very young, Easy to say, easy to play *and its accompanying CD. She lives in Kent with her husband and two children.*

Published by
The Bible Reading Fellowship
First Floor, Elsfield Hall,
15–17 Elsfield Way, Oxford OX2 8FG
ISBN 1 84101 135 5

First published 2001
10 9 8 7 6 5 4 3 2 1

Acknowledgments
Unless otherwise stated, scripture quotations are taken from the Good News Bible published by The Bible Societies/HarperCollins Publishers Ltd, UK © American Bible Society 1966, 1971, 1976, 1992, used with permission.

A catalogue record for this book is available from the British Library

Printed and bound in Malta by Gutenberg Press Ltd

Easy ways to BIBLE FUN for the Very Young

Vicki Howie

Twelve Bible-based activities for 3–5s

CONTENTS

Friendly fun-filled
meetings for parents or
carers and pre-school
children with Bible-based
stories and activities
at
on
between
contact:
Refreshments

Introduction

Quite rightly, you want to make your regular church meetings for parents (or childminders) and their pre-school children different from any other coffee mornings. Perhaps you would like the children to have fun listening to a Bible story, singing songs, doing a simple craft activity and ending with a short prayer.

Or perhaps you teach under-fives at school or playschool and you would like to know how to link a Bible story (or morning assembly) with the everyday topics that you regularly teach, such as shapes and sizes, the weather, telling the time, counting and so on.

If so, then this book has been written for you. It provides twelve themed sessions for the busy church worker or teacher, each based on a Bible story, but made relevant to young children, under the following headings:

- Me
- Me and you
- At home
- Out and about

Only a small amount of preparation is required (outlined in the 'Ready, Steady, Go!' section at the beginning of each session). Simply take the book to each meeting or lesson and work from it, using the headings as your crib-sheet.

How the book works

You may like to have 'Storytime' at the same time of day or at the same time in each meeting. If parents or carers are present, this time could perhaps be when the adults have finished their coffee and the children want a break from playing. Put some of the toys away so that the children are not distracted by them. Encourage the children to sit around you on rugs, with the adults (if present) seated in a semi-circle behind them. Don't worry if some children would prefer to sit on their parents' laps.

Use the 'Welcome' section to remind yourself to give everyone a warm welcome to the group. (Don't let anyone come in and sit on their own.) Space has been left for you to write in the name of any newcomers or any speaker, so that you can introduce them to your regular group. (You may like to sing the song 'You are welcome' from *Feeling Good!* published by Church House Publishing, a collection of simple songs written especially for younger children.)

The 'Theme' paragraph reminds you to tell the adults about the day's theme and helps you to explain the meaning of the Bible story that they will hear being read to the children.

Fill in any 'Notices' in advance, in the space provided. Use this opportunity to tell everyone about a new baby, to publicize church events and to remind them of the next meeting.

The children will thoroughly enjoy singing 'Happy Birthday' to anyone with a birthday close to this meeting. Find out their names during coffee time and write them down in the space provided. Singing the song is a good way to gain the children's attention, so be ready with Teddy and your story basket immediately afterwards.

Teddy and the story basket

You will find it much easier to entertain the children and hold their attention if you use a teddy (or other soft toy character) each week to help you tell the simple story based on the objects you have brought in your story basket or story box (see below). You could give him the same name as your group (for example, Rainbow Teddy, First Steps Teddy, Sunbeam Teddy). The children will identify with Teddy as he learns all about God's wonderful world and asks the questions that they may be too shy to ask. If you are at all shy yourself about being in the limelight, you will find that Teddy will draw everyone's attention away from you—their eyes will be on him.

Make Teddy as lovable, mischievous and comical as you can—rather like a small child. Practise with him at home, making him jump up and down, wave at the children, look in the basket and whisper in your ear. (If you have any doll's clothes or baby clothes of the right size, dress him in different clothes each time to suit your theme.)

Find an intriguing story basket or box with a lid in which to bring the objects suggested in the 'Ready' section. A traditional picnic hamper basket is ideal because you can keep the buckles done up and the contents hidden from the children until you are ready to show them. The children will soon get to know that the story basket contains all sorts of exciting toys and visual aids and they will be eager to sit by you waiting for you to say, 'I wonder what's in the story basket today!' Intrigue them; keep them guessing! Open the lid a fraction and peep in yourself. 'Oh, I can see someone furry... with a long, long tail... and a whiskery nose...Would you like to see? Yes, it's a *(bringing out the toy)* MOUSE!'

The 'story basket story' has been especially written to prepare the children for hearing the interactive Bible story. However, if you have very young children in the group, you may choose to use the story basket only. If so, the words in bold at the end of the paragraph will help you to make this story complete in itself.

Try to encourage any adults present to join in with the songs. It is quite acceptable to sing nursery rhymes and general songs familiar to everyone, especially when they provide a neat link with your theme. For example, *Incy Wincy Spider* is not a specifically Christian song, but a spider is part of God's creation and could link in with a session about the weather.

The song books suggested here are *Okki-tokki-unga*, *Apusskidu* and *Carol, gaily carol* (all published by A&C Black), *Feeling Good!* (published by the National Society/Church House Publishing) and *Junior Praise Combined Edition* (published by Marshall Pickering). Suggested songs other than in these books are well known and traditional and should be easy to locate in compilation song books for very young children/pianists. You might also wish to have a selection of tapes of Christian songs, such as *Little Kids' Praise* (Spring Harvest), available from your local Christian bookshop.

The 'play-acting' section is really aimed at children who are just starting at school, rather than toddlers. They will have fun trying out the mimes and this will help them to be thinking along the right lines before you read them the Bible story.

The 'Bible story' has been especially written for you to read aloud to the children. Show them the pictures as you do so. You may photocopy and enlarge the illustrations if you wish to use them as colouring-in sheets. The stories are interactive, with suggested mimes to help bring the stories alive. Encourage the children to repeat the words written in bold text (usually amusing words or important phrases). The children will be able to participate more on a second reading.

The 'craft' page can be photocopied and given to the children to colour or decorate. It can be taken home and displayed as a reminder of everything they have learned in the session.

The 'prayer' is short and simple, tying together all the elements of the session and making them relevant to the children. In a church group, ask different (willing) adults to read out the prayer each time as a way of including them in the session. (You may find new storytellers or committee members!) Explain to the children that prayer is simply talking to God, but try to instil in them a sense of wonder that the one who made our world is listening to us. Encourage them to keep still and quiet, with their eyes shut and their hands together, for this short time. You may like to introduce the prayer with the traditional rhyme:

Teddy bear, Teddy bear,
Turn around.
Teddy bear, Teddy bear,
Touch the ground.

Teddy bear, Teddy bear,
Climb the stairs.
Teddy bear, Teddy bear,
Say your prayers!

Ready, Steady, Go!

Where do you begin? First of all, look at the Contents page on page 5 for an appropriate topic. Then...

Ready! Pack the story basket with the items suggested. Try to make sure that these are colourful and appealing to young children. (Some of the parents in your group may be able to lend you toys if you do not have appropriate items yourself.)

Steady! Take the time to read the Bible verses on which the material is based. It will help to focus your mind on the points you want to put across. (The Bible story is based on the first Bible reference on the list.)

Go! You're ready to provide some Bible fun for the very young!

Don't forget to advertise the dates, time and place of your meetings by photocopying and enlarging the poster on page 6. Put posters in your local shops, the library and the health centre as well as on your church notice boards. Give one to whoever runs the baptism preparation classes so that they can recommend your group to the families they meet.

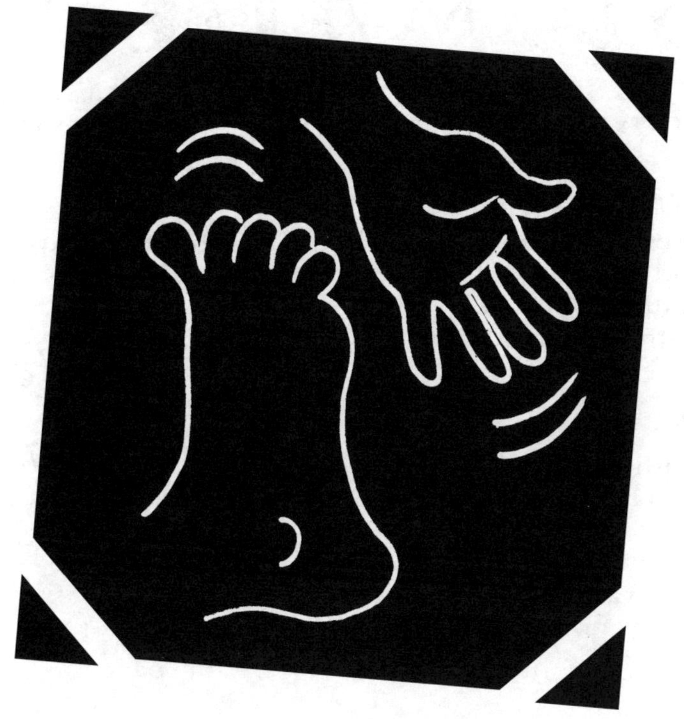

Me

ONE, TWO, THREE... GOD MADE ME!

Introduction

In this session, the children have fun wiggling their fingers and toes and learning who gave them their wonderful bodies. They hear how God made Adam and Eve in the Bible story.

Ready...

- Pack the story basket with a child's colourful knitted glove, sock and hat taped at intervals to the end of a big ball of colourful wool.
- Wind some brightly coloured wool around your fingers and cut into various lengths for the hair in the craft activity, or take Plasticine for modelling.

Steady...

Read: Genesis 2:4b–23
Psalm 139:13–14
Luke 12:6–7

Go...

You're ready to explain that God made us and that we are all very special to him.

Let's begin!

Welcome

Welcome everyone! Especially...

Theme

Explain today's theme to the adults, if present. As God's children, we are a very special part of creation. We can start to get some idea about how special we are to God, when we think how much our own children mean to us.

Notices

Sing Happy Birthday to

The story basket

Sit with Teddy and the ball of wool on your lap, the end of the wool leading mysteriously into the basket.

Say, *'Robert, that's a lovely jumper you're wearing. Did Mummy knit it for you? Teddy has been doing some knitting today!'* (Hold up the wool.) *'Would you like to see what he's made?'* Ask an eager child to come and pull on the wool until the glove appears. *'What's that? Does it go on your foot? No? On your head? Oh no, of course not! A glove keeps your hand and fingers warm. Try it on! Who made our fingers? Can you count them? Can you wiggle them? Who made our hands? Can you clap them?'*

Repeat with the knitted sock (wiggle toes) and the hat (nod heads). Ask the children if they can count all the hairs on their heads. Some will probably come up with an answer. Tell them that only God knows the right answer. He has counted every single hair because…

…he made us and he loves us so much.

Suggested songs

Heads, shoulders, knees and toes (*Okki-tokki-unga*)

The body song (*Feeling Good!*)

From my knees to my nose (*Junior Praise*)

Any action song would be appropriate, since this will involve moving parts of the body. You could draw funny faces on your fingers, and then sing (to the tune, 'One, two, three, four, five'):

One, two, three, four, five
(count fingers),
Make your fingers come alive
(wiggle fingers),
Six, seven, eight, nine, ten
(count fingers again),
They can bend and stretch again!
(bend and stretch fingers)

Play-acting

Ask everyone to lie on the floor, as quiet and as still as possible. Then gradually 'come alive' by wiggling toes, shaking legs, waving arms, and so on, until everyone jumps up and shouts, 'One, two, three, God made me!'

Craft

Let the children colour the portrait and then help them to glue on the wool hair. Put some small mirrors on the table so that they can copy their own hairstyles and generally admire themselves.

Or, give the children some Plasticine and help them to model people and animals.

Prayer

Ask ______________________ to read today's prayer.

Thank you, God, that you made me,
That I'm as special as can be!
Thank you, God, for loving me so,
From the top of my head to the tip of each toe.
Amen

One, two, three, God made me!

The world was just a few days old. Big, soft leaves glowed in the sunshine. The sea sparkled. And baby animals played in the jungle.

'I *am* pleased with my wonderful, new world,' said God.

'And I'm very pleased with all the animals I made to live in it.

Can you see my shy little creature with a long, thin tail and a whiskery nose?'

Squeak, squeak!

'And look at that hairy creature with the swing-along arms and very clever toes!'

Oo, oo!

'Listen to the feathery, beaky creature singing at the top of the tree.'

Chirrup, chirrup!

'And see how that big, black, shiny creature can jump right out of the sea.'

Ker-splosh!

'That's all very good,' said God to himself. 'But I haven't finished yet. I'm going to make someone who could talk to me, someone who could walk with me, especially in the sunshine after tea.'

God bent down and scooped up some warm, brown earth. For a moment, he rocked it like a baby in his big, gentle hands. Then, with two nods of his head...

...nod, nod...

...he set to work.

His clever fingers stroked the earth, pushing and patting it into different shapes in the palm of each hand. The earth grew warmer and easier to model.

'I'm making a man to look after you,' God told the animals.

'I'm giving him fingers and toes... ears, eyes and a nose... shoulders, knees and elbows... and I will call him Adam, and I will love him and we will be the very best of friends.'

The man lay finished and perfect in God's hands. He was quite still. Not a finger wiggled. Not a toe twitched... until God took a deep breath...

...oohhmm...

...and blew the dust from his hands...

...ppsshh!

Then, one, two, three...

'...God made me!' cried Adam. 'Hooray! I'm so pleased to be alive!' And he wiggled his warm, brown fingers...
...wiggle, wiggle...
...and he twitched his warm, brown toes...
...twitch, twitch!

Adam walked with God and talked with God all the way to a beautiful garden at the edge of the jungle. When Adam saw all the apples and oranges and bananas growing on the trees, he clapped his hands...
...clap, clap!

'Can I climb the trees and pick the fruit?' he asked.

'Of course!' said God. 'You can even look after the garden for me. But please remember—don't touch the tree in the middle. That is a dangerous tree and the fruit is very bad for you.'

God brought all his creatures to meet Adam.

'Who would you like to keep you company in the garden?' he asked. 'What about the shy one with the whiskery nose?'
Squeak, squeak!

'But he's as quiet as a... as a mouse!' exclaimed Adam.

'That's a very good name for him!' said God. 'Then what about the hairy creature with swing-along arms and clever toes?'
Oo, oo!

'But he's a little monkey,' laughed Adam. 'And he's much too noisy! I really need someone a bit more like me!'

God waited until Adam was fast asleep. Then, very gently, he took one of Adam's ribs in his clever hands. And he used it to make him a wife. She had fingers and toes... ears, eyes and a lovely upturned nose... And when he saw her, Adam said...

'One, two, three... God made you and me!'

After tea, they all walked and they talked and God was very, very pleased. For he loved them both from the tops of their heads to the tips of their toes!

One, two, three, God made me!

I'M ONLY SMALL...

Introduction

In this session, the children think about the different sizes of objects and people around them—big, small, long, short and tall—before they listen to the story of David and Goliath.

Ready...

- Pack the story basket with some interesting objects of different sizes for the children to compare.
- You could take some toy animals: for example, a small mouse, a big elephant, a tall giraffe, and a long animal doorstop; or a pair of baby's shoes, a pair of child's sandals and a pair of adult's shoes (giant's size!).

Steady...

Read: 1 Samuel 17:1–50
Ephesians 6:10–11

Go...

You're ready to show that though we may sometimes feel frightened and small, knowing that God is with us can help us 'walk tall'!

Let's begin!

Welcome

Welcome everyone! Especially...

Theme

Explain today's theme to the adults, if present. The Bible story today is about a small boy who overcame a giant. Although we don't have to fight giants, we often face situations in life that make us feel small and helpless. However, if we remember that God is with us and that 'the battle is the Lord's', we gain the courage to tackle our own particular Goliaths!

Notices

Sing Happy Birthday to

The story basket

Explain that Teddy has brought some of his toys (or whatever you have chosen) for the children to look at, and that they are all different sizes.

Gradually bring out the objects and talk about size: for example, *'Look, here's a giraffe and he's very... tall! What's this? A mouse, and he's very... small!'* and so on. (If you are using the shoes, bring out the baby's pair first and say, *'I think these belong to someone very small...'* and so on.)

Ask the children to look all around the room. Say, *'I can see some tall people... and some small people... and some even smaller baby people.'*

In school, you could measure the children on a height chart.

God has made us in all different sizes, and he loves us and helps us whether we're tall or small.

Suggested songs

The three bears (*Okki-tokki-unga*)
On my tiptoes I am tall (*Little Kids' Praise*)
Jesus' love is very wonderful (*Junior Praise*)
My God is so big (*Junior Praise*)
Only a boy called David (*Junior Praise*)

Play-acting

Tell the children about something that gave you a fright when you were small. (Choose something comical and not very frightening.) Explain that it made your knees go wobbly like jelly.

Ask the children whether they have ever been frightened by something, before encouraging them to act out this poem:

When your knobbly knees are shaking...
(wobble knees)
And you feel afraid and small...
(crouch down)
That's the time
To say this rhyme,
Be brave... chin up...
(push chin up with hand)
... grow tall!
(stand up and stretch arms up)

When you have read the story of David and Goliath to the children, you may like to say these rhymes to them. Encourage everyone to do the simple actions and to shout out 'boo!' and 'shoo!' If you have some confident older ones in the group, they could take turns at playing David, the lion and the bear.

Up on a hill,
The boy David sat still...
(all sit, David on a chair)
Watching his little lambs play...
(all shade eyes and look around)
A lion (or 'big bear') said, 'BOO!'
(animal pops up from behind chair)
But David went, 'SHOO!'
(all shoo away with hands)
And frightened the lion (or 'big bear') away!
(animal disappears again)

Craft

When the children have coloured in the picture, help them to fold it so that the child appears to be sitting on the giraffe. Now say the words at the top and unfold the paper to make the characters grow tall.

Prayer

Ask ____________________ to read today's prayer.

Dear God,
You are so big and so strong.
Whenever I feel afraid and small,
I just remember that you are looking after me,
And then I feel nine feet tall! Thank you, God!
Amen

I'm only small...

There was once a small boy called David who had seven big brothers. What a big family!

Everything his brothers did, David wanted to do too!

One day, the biggest brothers went away to fight in a battle.

'Can I come too?' asked David.

The brothers shook their heads.

Shake, shake!

'You're much too small to fight in a battle,' they said. 'You must stay at home and look after the sheep. But look out for hungry lions and bears. They would like to eat the little lambs, and they would like to eat you too!'

'Don't worry!' said David. 'I'm only small but God is big and strong... *(flex muscles)* and he will help me do anything at all—even look after the sheep!'

David sat on the hillside playing his harp.

Twing, twang!

And then he fired stones from his catapult.

Bing, bang!

And while he was busy, who should come prowling through the bushes on big furry paws, licking his lips and sharpening his claws, but a huge, horrible, hungry...

... LION!

Roar!

And he snatched a little lamb—just like that!

'Give me back my lamb,' shouted David, 'or I'll shake you till your teeth rattle!'

The lion opened his big mouth and roared with laughter.

'Ha ha ha!'

'Why, you're only a boy! I could pin you to the floor with just one paw!'

'Ha ha ha!'

'I may be small,' said David. 'But God is big and strong... *(flex muscles)* and he will help me do anything at all—even fight a lion!'

And he took the lion by the scruff of his neck and shook him until his teeth went...

...jingle, jangle...

...and he dropped the frightened lamb.

David was so pleased that he played a 'thank you' song to God on his harp.

Twing, twang!

And he fired some more stones with his catapult.

Bing, bang!

And while he was busy, who should come prowling through the bushes on big furry paws, licking his lips and sharpening his claws, but a big, brown, beastly...

… BEAR!

Growl!

And he snatched a little lamb—just like that!

'Give me back my lamb,' shouted David, 'or I'll shake you till your teeth rattle!'

The bear opened his big mouth and gave a growly laugh.

'Ha ha ha!'

'Why, you're only a boy! I could pin you to the floor with just one paw!'

'Ha ha ha!'

'I may be small,' said David, 'but God is big and strong… *(flex muscles).* He helped me fight a lion and now he will help me fight a bear!'

And he grabbed the bear by the scruff of his neck and shook him until his teeth went…

…jingle jangle…

…and he dropped the frightened lamb.

David went to visit his big brothers at the battle to tell them the sheep were quite safe. But while they were busy talking, who should come stamping through the bushes with a great big spear… *not* a roaring lion and *not* a growling bear, but…

…a great big giant called Goliath!

'Who will come and fight me?' bellowed the giant.

The big brothers felt very small. But David looked up at the giant and said, 'I will fight you.' Just like that!

Goliath opened his great big mouth and laughed.

'Ha ha ha!'

'Why, you're only a boy! I could squeeze you into sand with just one hand.'

'Ha ha ha!'

'I may be small,' said David, 'but God is big and strong… *(flex muscles).* He helped me fight a lion and he helped me fight a bear and now he will help me to fight you!'

And he fired a small stone from his catapult straight at Goliath.

BANG!

'Hooray! The giant is dead!' shouted the brothers and they lifted David up high on to their shoulders.

'Even though I'm very small,' sang David happily, 'God makes me feel nine feet tall!'

Twing, twang!

Craft Sheet

I DON'T FEEL VERY WELL!

Introduction

Use this session to encourage the children to feel sympathy for anyone who isn't well, and to appreciate good health. You could talk about the people who look after us when we are ill, before reading them the Bible story in which Jesus heals Jairus' daughter.

Ready...

- Pack the story basket with some dolls' pillows and blankets, a doctor's or nurse's outfit and bag, and a small cup.
- Take a shoebox as a bed for Teddy.

Steady...

Read: Luke 8:40–56

Go...

You're ready to explain that Jesus can always help us, however bad things may seem.

Let's begin!

Welcome

Welcome everyone! Especially...

Theme

Explain today's theme to the adults, if present. Mention anyone who is away through illness. Every parent knows how worrying it is when their child is ill. We may feel helpless, but the Bible story reminds us that we can always bring Jesus into the situation with a prayer.

Notices

Sing Happy Birthday to

The story basket

Tell the children that Teddy is usually a very happy bear. In the mornings, he jumps out of bed (make him do all these actions), stretches his arms up to the ceiling and then down to the floor, washes his face, eats a big breakfast and then brushes his teeth. BUT today poor Teddy doesn't feel very well. His head aches and his tummy aches and all he wants to do is to get into bed. Say, '*Have you ever felt unwell? What was the matter?*' Ask the children to make Teddy as comfortable as they can in his bed with the pillow and blankets. '*Are you feeling better now, Teddy? No, his head still hurts...*' and so on. '*Perhaps we should call a doctor.*'

Let several confident children use the doctor's kit, listening to his chest and pretending to give him some water to drink. Now Teddy feels much better and he jumps out of bed. Thank the children for looking after Teddy.

Jesus takes good care of us when we are sick and he wants us to be kind to anyone we know who is not well.

Suggested songs

A-ring-a-ring of roses
Humpty Dumpty
Miss Polly (*Okki-tokki-unga*)
I jump out of bed in the morning (*Okki-tokki-unga*)
Wake up and praise the Lord (*Little Kids' Praise*)
Jesus' hands were kind hands (*Junior Praise*)

Play-acting

Ask the children to lie on the floor with their eyes closed as if they are in bed. Mime waking up, sitting up, stretching and yawning, then jumping out of bed and shouting, 'Thank you, God, for this wonderful day!'

Craft

When the children have coloured the pictures of the little girl and her bed, help them to slot the girl into the bed where shown. Then jump her out of bed! Alternatively, help the children to make 'Get well' cards for anyone they know who is ill.

Prayer

Ask ______________________ to read today's prayer.

Dear God,
Thank you for all the people who look after me when I don't feel very well.
Please help all the kind doctors and nurses who work at the surgery and in the hospital.
Thank you, God, that you are always taking care of me! ***Amen***

I don't feel very well!

Who's that sleeping in the little bed?
It's a little girl.
It's Jairus' little girl.
She should be up by now.
The sun is up.
Her mother is up getting the breakfast.
Jairus, her father, is up getting dressed.
What's the matter with the little girl?
Her head hurts... *(rub heads),*
Her tummy aches... *(rub tummies),*
She doesn't feel very well.
Poor little girl!

Jairus strokes his little girl's head.
She is hot. Her cheeks are very red.
Her mother brings her some water to drink.
But the little girl pushes it away.
Her head still hurts... *(rub head),*
And her tummy still aches...*(rub tummies),*
Poor little girl!

'What shall we do?' asks her mother.
'We'll fetch Jesus,' says her father.
'That's what we'll do!'

Jairus hurries out into the sunshine.
'Where's Jesus?' he calls.
The neighbours point to the beach.
Jairus runs along the dusty road.
It seems such a long way!
And the road is very busy today.
Where's Jesus? There's Jesus!
He's talking to all the people by the lake.
Jairus kneels down at his feet.
'My little girl is dying!' he says.
'*Please* come and make her better.'
'Poor little girl!' says Jesus.

Jesus comes to the little girl's house.
The neighbours are outside, crying and wailing.
'The little girl is dead!' they say.
Poor little girl!

'Don't worry!' says Jesus. 'She is only sleeping.'
He takes the little girl's hand.
'It's time to get up!' he says.
And the little girl jumps out of bed!
She dances around the room.
Her mother and father cannot believe their eyes.
'Bring her something to eat!' laughs Jesus.
'Now she's a happy little, hungry little girl!'

Craft Sheet

Jump out of bed and say, 'Thank you, God, for this wonderful day!'

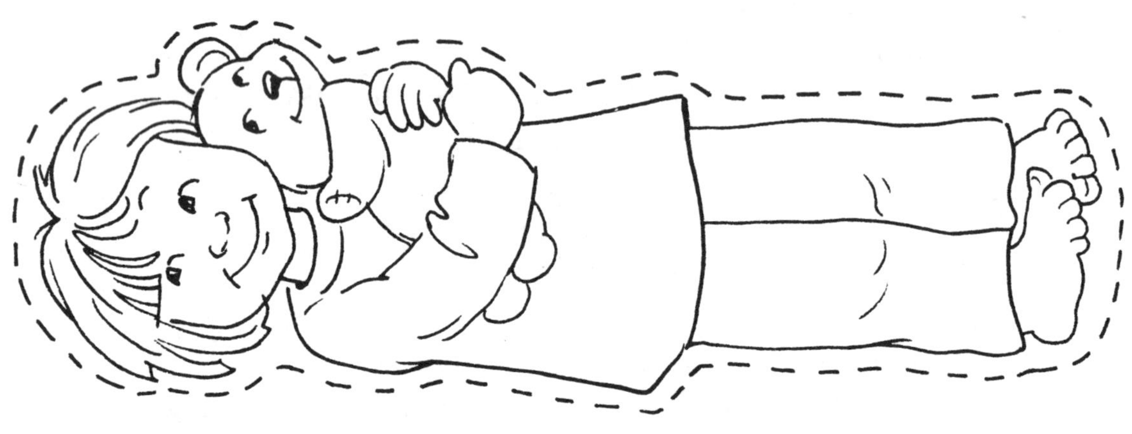

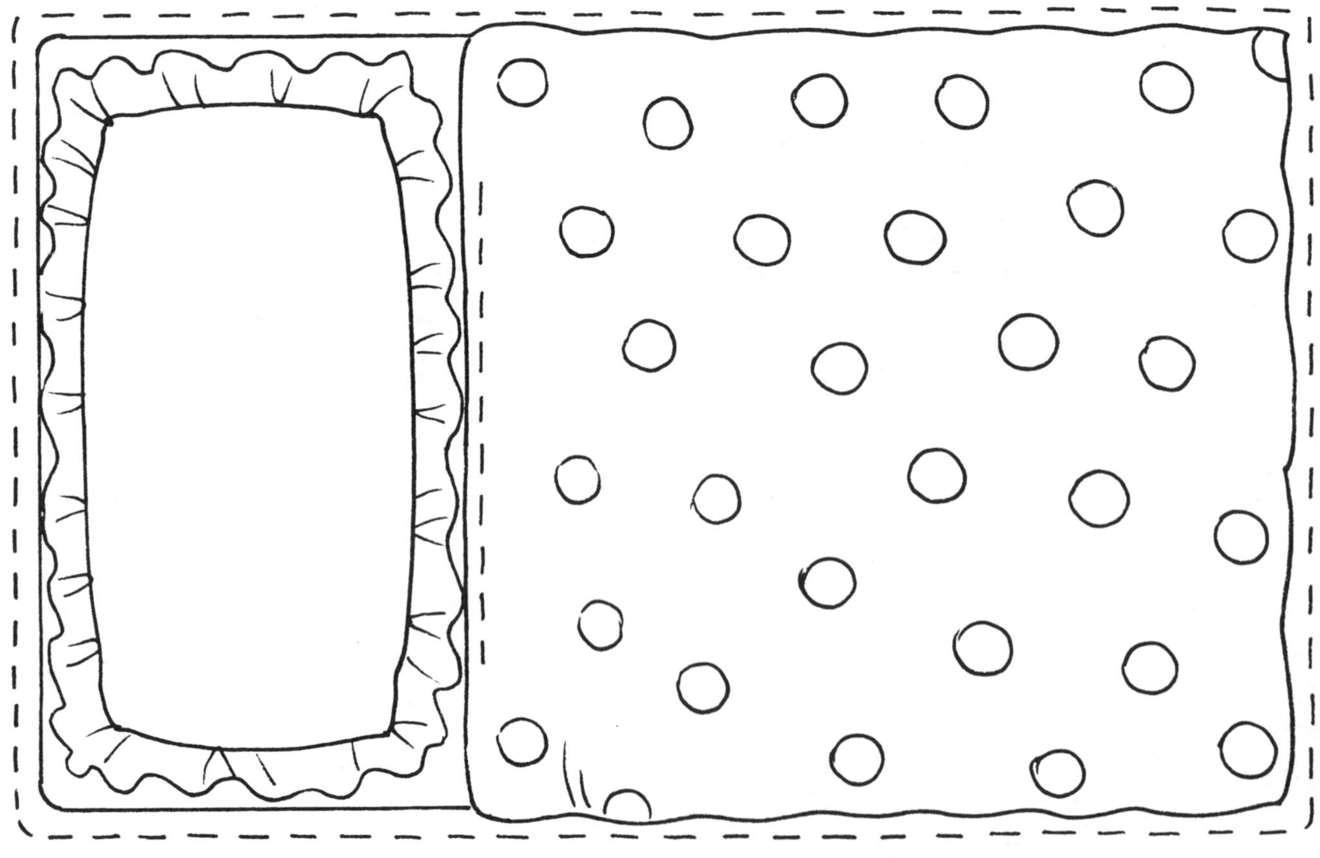

Me and you

I'M SORRY!

Introduction

In this session, the children learn the importance of saying 'sorry', before they listen to the story of the prodigal son.

Ready...

- Pack the story basket with a small blackboard (or wipe-clean memo pad), some chalk and a duster, or a selection of farm animals (including a pig) from a toy farm for the children to examine.

Steady...

Read: Luke 15:11–32

Go...

You're ready to put across the image of God as a wonderfully loving father, always ready to forgive us and to let us start all over again whenever we are truly sorry.

Let's begin!

Welcome

Welcome everyone! Especially...

Theme

If you are using this session at the beginning of a new term or particularly at the start of a new year, show the adults a new diary or calendar and ask them whether they have made any new year or new term resolutions. Do they think they will keep them up all year/term?

We can never hope to be perfect, but point out that while there are only a few opportunities during the calendar year to start afresh, God is always ready to let us start all over again. He wipes the slate clean if we are truly sorry and really want to do better.

Notices

Sing Happy Birthday to

The story basket

Sit with Teddy on your lap. Tell the children that you are very sorry to say that Teddy is being naughty today.

Make up some naughty but comical things that Teddy has done. (If the children volunteer some information about their own naughty behaviour, congratulate them on owning up and ask them if they remembered to say sorry.)

Ask Teddy to sit quietly while you draw a simple picture of an animal (a pig) on the board for the children to identify. When they have named it correctly, make Teddy grab the chalk and scribble all over the pig! *'Naughty Teddy! You've spoilt the picture and you've made all the children feel sad!'*

Teddy says he is sorry. *'Never mind, we'll forget all about that now'* (rubbing out the mess) *'and we'll start all over again.'*

It makes God sad when we do naughty things but he is happy when we say 'sorry' and he lets us make a new start.

Suggested songs

Old Macdonald had a farm
Where, oh where has my little dog gone? (see 'Play-acting' below)
S/he'll be coming round the mountain (Oh, we'll all go out and meet him when he comes... Oh, he'll have a brand new tunic when he comes... Oh, we'll give a great big party when he comes...) (*Apusskidu*)
The bear (boy) went over the mountain (*Apusskidu*)
I'm sorry (*Feeling Good!*)
Sometimes I'm naughty (*Junior Praise*)

Play-acting

With very young children, do the finger rhyme 'Two little dicky birds sitting on a wall' to introduce the idea of going away and coming back again.

Older children could mime taking a boisterous dog for a walk. He pulls on the lead... so they let him off... and watch him disappear into the distance. Now they are happy to see him coming back... and they run to give him a hug and a pat.

Craft

Let the children colour the picture and help them to write the words 'I'm sorry!'

Prayer

Ask ______________________________ to read today's prayer.

Dear God,
Sometimes we do things that make you sad.
Please help us to say 'sorry'.
Thank you that you always forgive us,
and let us start all over again. **Amen**

I'm sorry!

Do you ever feel so cross that you fold your arms... *(fold arms)*

...stamp your foot... *(stamp foot)* and shout,

'That's it! I'm off!'

Jesus told a story about a boy who did just that.

One morning, the boy woke up feeling as angry as a lion shut in a cage.

He sprang out of bed and flung on his old tunic and sandals.

Then he paced up and down, up and down. Out of the window, he could see his father and brother working hard on the farm.

'Hurry up!' they called. 'There's work to do!'

At this, the boy folded his arms... stamped his foot... and roared,

'That's it! I'm off!'

The boy marched out and spoke rudely to his father.

'Look at me! I'm nearly grown up,' he said.

'Give me my money! I'm going to leave home!'

The father loved his boy and he wanted him to stay.

But he let him go.

'Here's your money,' he said sadly.

'Please be careful, and don't forget to wave when you reach the top of that hill.'

'Hooray! I'm free!' sang the boy as he skipped up the hillside.

He was so busy jingling his money that he quite forgot to look back and wave.

The boy reached a busy town. The market was full of exciting things to buy.

'Now I can have anything I want!' he exclaimed.

He dipped into his moneybag over and over again.

Soon the bag was empty. Soon his tummy was empty, too!

'I'm hungry,' said the boy. 'I'd better get a job.'

Someone gave him a job looking after some pigs.

But no one gave him any food!

'Look at me!' he snorted. 'I'm so cold and hungry, I could eat the pigs' dinner!'

Then he hugged himself to keep warm... stamped his feet... and said,

'That's it! I'm going home!'

'Perhaps my father will give me a job on the farm.'

The boy turned back towards his home. When he reached the top of the hill, his father saw him coming and ran to give him a hug.

'Oh, Dad,' cried the boy. 'I'm so sorry!'

'Never mind about that now,' laughed his father.

'We must find you a new tunic and some new shoes. Then we'll have a party!'

When the boy's brother came in from the farm he folded his arms... stamped his foot... and shouted, **'I don't believe it! That runaway doesn't deserve a party!'**

'Oh, please come and join in!' begged the father. 'I was sad when your brother went away. But now I am happy because he said sorry.'

Jesus said that God celebrates whenever we say sorry! HOORAY!

Craft Sheet

Don't forget to say

Memos

I'm sorry

LET'S SHARE!

Introduction

Sharing is something that young children find very difficult to do. In this session, the children enjoy sharing Teddy's birthday picnic, before they hear about the little lad who shared *his* picnic in the story of the feeding of the five thousand.

Ready...

- Pin a birthday badge on Teddy.
- Pack the story basket with a rug, a doll's tea-set or some birthday paper cups and plates, a packet of sponge fingers or iced biscuits and a bottle of prepared squash.
- Or, pack items for the children to count, such as the beads on an abacus, toy bricks or some items taken from the Bible story.
- Take some 'hundreds and thousands' used for cake decoration for the craft activity.

Steady...

Read: John 6:1–14
Luke 6:38
1 Timothy 6:17–19

Go...

You're ready to put over the great happiness to be found in sharing with others.

Let's begin!

Welcome

Welcome everyone! Especially...

Theme

Explain to any adults present that today's theme is 'sharing'. New mums and dads may find it comforting to know that it is not just *their* toddler who refuses to share his toys! Express the hope that parents at the group can form friendships and share any worries about their children. Point out that God wants us to share both our worries and our joys with him.

Notices

Sing Happy Birthday to

The story basket

Ask the children whether they can see anything special about Teddy… Point out Teddy's badge and explain that it is Teddy's birthday today. Say, *'You must be very happy, Teddy.'* (Make him shake his head.) *'No? But why not?'* (Teddy whispers in your ear.) Explain that Teddy has brought a delicious birthday picnic with him in the story basket but he has no one to share it with. *'Oh, dear! But just a minute… perhaps you would like to have a birthday picnic with Teddy.'*

Get the children to help you spread out the rug, and give everyone a cup and plate. Explain that Teddy is going to share his food and drink, but that first you are all going to sing a song to say 'thank you' for the food. (After the song, make Teddy hand out the food and drink.) *'Now let's see if Teddy is happy.'* (Teddy jumps up and down.) *'Yes! Teddy is very, very happy because he likes to share with his friends.'*

And God wants us to share, because he knows that will make everyone happy!

Suggested songs

The teddy bear's picnic
Pat-a-cake, pat-a-cake, baker's man
Any form of sung Grace (see below)
Fish and bread (*Feeling Good!*)
Share it round (*Feeling Good!*)

A 'thank you' song

One, two, three, four, five,
Thank you that I am alive!
Six, seven, eight, nine, ten,
Thank you for my food, Amen.

Play-acting

Use this rhyme as an introduction to the story. You could hide five bread rolls and two fish shapes covered in silver foil in the basket for everyone to find at the end! Ask if this would be enough to feed everyone.

One, two, buckle my shoe
(mime fastening shoe),
Three, four, run down to the shore
(run on the spot),
Five, six, pick up pebbles and sticks
(mime gathering),
Seven, eight, it's getting late
(tap wrists),
Nine, ten, I'm hungry again
(rub tummies),
Eleven, twelve, in the basket delve
(all run to look in basket)!

Craft

When the children have coloured the teddy bear's picnic picture, help them to put glue on the cake and then sprinkle it with the hundreds and thousands! As you do this, talk to them about the food, games and toys they may have shared at their own birthday parties or picnics.

Prayer

Ask ______________________________ to read today's prayer.

Dear God,
Thank you for my favourite toy,
and the pictures in my books.
Thank you for a juicy drink
and the food that Mummy cooks.
Thank you, God, for all the fun
when I share all this with everyone. ***Amen***

Let's share!

One small boy sees out of his window,
Two silver fish lying in a fishing net,
Three sails flapping on a boat across the water.
'Mummy, is it time for our picnic yet?'

'Four more minutes is all you have to wait, dear,
Five little barley loaves I've made for you and me.
Put on your sandals and bring me your basket,
I want to pack the silver fish and bread for our tea.'

One small boy buckles up his sandals,
Two hands carry the basket to the sea,
Three excited children are pointing at the water.
'Someone special's in that boat—who can it be?'

Four splashing waves bring the boat to the water's edge,
Jesus steps ashore, he's the one we've come to see.
Five thousand people on the beach have come to meet him.
'Let's listen to Lord Jesus before we have our tea.'

One small boy stands listening to Jesus,
Two little feet in the water getting wet,
Three happy children say, 'We want another story!'
(The picnic's in the basket, it's not been eaten yet.)

Soon four little stars are twinkling in the evening sky,
Five thousand people are still sitting by the sea.
'Who can find some food to feed the hungry people?
Who has a picnic that they can share with me?'

One small boy wants to share his picnic,
Two little hands hold up the fish and barley bread,
Three hungry children wait together on the grassy hill.
'Thank you, God,' says Jesus, 'that all these people will be fed.'

Four little birds fly down for crumbs left over,
Five thousand people have picnicked by the sea,
One small boy whispers, 'Jesus must be special,
He fed one, two, three, four, five thousand people with my tea!'

Craft Sheet

WITH LOVE FROM ME TO YOU!

Introduction

In this session, the children learn about the best Christmas present of all—Jesus, God's gift to each one of us. The nativity story could be used as the basis for a very simple nativity play.

Ready...

- Pack the story basket with a Postman Pat van, a signed Christmas card in an envelope for each child depicting a character or characters from the nativity story (shepherds, angels, animals, a star and so on), and a baby doll wrapped in brown paper and string. Attach a label that reads 'With love from me to you'.

Steady...

Read: Matthew 1:18–24 and Luke 2:1–20
John 3:16

Go...

You're ready to explain that God loves every one of us so much that he sent us his very own Son at the first Christmas.

Let's begin!

Welcome

Welcome everyone! Especially...

Theme

Point out to any adults present that the Christmas story is full of messages from God to human beings, brought by the angels. The message is JESUS! Although the story is so familiar, we can each discover a new message from God if we listen carefully to its retelling in readings, carols and plays this Christmas.

Notices

Sing Happy Birthday to

The story basket

Explain to the children that Teddy is feeling very happy because it is nearly Christmas *(jump him up and down)*. He loves to look out for the postman because he often brings Christmas cards with messages from Teddy's friends and parcels from people who love him. I wonder if the postman is going to come to us today! Bring out the van and ask Teddy to help deliver a card to each child.

When they have all opened their cards, you could sing the 'Postman Pat' song to regain their attention. Say, '*Who has an angel on their card? Who has a shepherd looking after his sheep?*' and so on. Explain that all these characters and animals will be in the story today.

'*But wait a minute! The postman is knocking at the door! Rat-a-tat-tat! There's a parcel for Teddy to open!*' Read the label out loud and ask the children to help Teddy undo the paper and string to reveal the baby doll. Explain that **Christmas is a happy time because God sent us his Son, baby Jesus, at the very first Christmas long ago.**

Suggested songs

Songs and carols
'Postman Pat' song
Christmas is a happy time (*Feeling Good!*)
A baby was born (*Feeling Good!*)
Rat-a-tat-tat, rat-a-tat-tat! (*Carol, gaily carol*)
Away in a manger

Play-acting

Ask the children to find a partner. One child mimes wrapping a great big parcel, tying a bow and writing a label. They give it to their partner, saying, 'With love from me to you!' This child mimes unwrapping the parcel and finding a present inside. You could explain the importance of saying 'Thank you'.

Craft

As the children decorate the present tag, ask them if they plan to use it on a present for someone special.

Prayer

Ask ______________________ to read today's prayer.

Dear God,
When I look at baby Jesus,
lying in the manger,
I know that you must love me very much,
to send me such a wonderful Christmas present!
Glory be to God! ***Amen***

With love from me to you!

God smiled down on the little town of Nazareth.

He could see Mary, singing as she sewed new clothes… *(mime sewing)*

…and Joseph, the carpenter, whistled as he sawed wood to make furniture *(mime sawing)*.

How God loved them both! How he loved everyone!

God called for the angel Gabriel. **'Gabriel!'**

'I am going to send the world a wonderful present,' said God.

'But I need Mary's help. Will you take a message to her?'

'Of course,' replied the angel. 'What shall I say?'

'Dear Mary,' began God. 'It's good news! You are going to have a baby boy. He is my own dear Son. Please call him Jesus! With love from God.'

The angel sparkled with excitement and went to call on Mary.

(Call) 'Mary!'

'Mary!'

'Now we must tell Joseph about the baby,' said God when the angel arrived back in heaven.

'Wait until he is asleep… *(heads on hands)*

…then whisper the good news into his dreams.'

(Call quietly) 'Joseph!'

'Joseph!'

God was pleased to see Mary and Joseph so happy.

Mary sewed tiny clothes for the baby… *(mime sewing)*

…and Joseph sawed wood for a tiny cot *(mime sawing)*.

But one day a soldier's voice echoed in the street.

'Listen, everybody!' he shouted.

(Shout) 'Listen, everybody!'

'Listen, everybody!'

'The emperor wants to count all his people.

You must return to the town that your family comes from.

Write your names on the register there.

This is the order of the Emperor, Augustus.'

'But that means Mary and Joseph will have to go all the way to Bethlehem,' gasped the angel Gabriel. 'And the baby is due at any moment!'

JESUS

Joseph led his little donkey into the yard.

He packed her baskets with food and rugs for the journey to Bethlehem.

Then he helped Mary up on to the donkey's back.

There was no room for the baby clothes or the new wooden cot.

God watched over them as they travelled by day.

And he looked after them as they slept out under the stars at night.

'Just look at all the people in Bethlehem!' exclaimed the angel Gabriel.

'All the inns are full! Wherever will they stay tonight?'

Mary and Joseph knocked on many doors... *(mime knocking)*

...and they called for the innkeeper.

(Call) 'Innkeeper!'

'Innkeeper!'

But each one said, 'No room! No room! No room!'

'Unless... would you like to shelter in my stable?'

'Yes, please!' chorused Mary and Joseph.

'Yes, please!'

'Good!' said God. 'Let a bright star shine above the stable!

It's time to send baby Jesus into the world.'

Mary and Joseph gazed at the tiny baby.

And they called him... Jesus...

Jesus...

...just as the angel had said.

Mary held Jesus until her arms grew tired.

Then Joseph laid him on the straw in the wooden manger.

It was almost as good as the wooden cot!

'Gabriel!' said God. 'We must tell the world that the baby has arrived.

Will you take a message to the shepherds out in the fields?

You may take a choir of angels to help you!'

'Of course!' said Gabriel. 'I know what to say!'

(Call) 'Shepherds!'

'Shepherds!'

As soon as the shepherds heard the good news, they came running to find the stable.

'The angel told us about the baby,' they explained.

'Glory be to God!'

'Glory be to God!'

Then God smiled down on that stable in the little town of Bethlehem.

He knew that baby Jesus would grow up to tell everyone the wonderful news that... God loves you!

God loves you!

With love from me to you!

At home

WONDERFUL WEATHER FOR WASHING!

Introduction

Use this session to talk about the different types of weather with the children, before going on to read them the story of the storm on the lake.

Ready...

- Take along a weather chart or make some simple weather symbols.
- Pack the story basket with some dolls' clothes, a washing-line and some pegs.
- Cut out the paper circles with their 'peep holes' for the children to make their own weather charts, and take some split-pin paper fasteners.

Steady...

Read: Mark 4:35–41
Psalm 91

Go...

You're ready to inspire the children with the thought that the powerful God who made and looks after the weather also takes care of us.

Let's begin!

Welcome

Welcome everyone! Especially...

Theme

If there are adults present, you could point out that life is rather like the weather. Sometimes the sun shines and everything seems to be going well. At other times, dark clouds blot out the sun and we sail right into a storm. When that happens, there is no need to panic. God is in control and he wants us to ask him for the help we need to sail on into calmer waters!

Notices

Sing Happy Birthday to

The story basket

Show the children your weather chart or symbols and ask them to find the pictures that match today's weather. Or you could ask them about their favourite weather. Say, *'Who likes to splash in puddles? Has anybody flown a kite in windy weather? Who has built a snowman?'*

Tell the children that Teddy likes to play outside whatever the weather! In fact, he has made his clothes very muddy playing football and he has given them a good wash in some soapy water. Let them look at all the clothes in the basket. Give the ends of the line to two adults to hold and ask the children to help Teddy to peg his clothes on the line. *'Now we need some windy weather to dry Teddy's clothes. Can you make a sound like the wind blowing? Whoooo! That's it! Let's see if we can make the washing flap about in the wind! ... No! We're not blowing hard enough! Let's blow even harder...'* and so on. (When the children are making a good sound, signal the adult helpers to make the line sway!)

'Hooray, now Teddy's clothes will soon be dry! But, oh dear, I think I heard thunder and it's starting to rain. Quick, everyone. Help Teddy take his washing off the line again! Who made the wind? Who made the rain?'

God made all the different sorts of weather and we can have fun in the wind, rain and sun!

Suggested songs

I hear thunder
Incy wincy spider
The sun has got his hat on
Calming the storm (*Feeling Good!*)
With Jesus in the boat (*Junior Praise*)

Play-acting

Ask the children to imagine that they are jumping or skipping over tiny waves at the water's edge. As the breeze gets up, the waves get bigger and the children have to jump higher! You could do this to taped music, gradually increasing the volume.

Use this rhyme to introduce the story:

I'm a little sailing boat, long and thin...
(stand tall, arms at sides)
Watch my sails blow out and in...
(flap arms)
When I see the waves jump... (jump)
hear me sing
Naughty waves, you CAN'T COME IN!
(waggle index finger)

Craft

As the children colour in the picture, talk to them about the positive aspects of all kinds of weather, even weather which we think of as bad. Help them to attach the paper circles to their weather charts using the split-pins and to use the peep holes to find the matching pictures.

Prayer

Ask ______________________ to read today's prayer.

Dear God,
Thank you, God, for fun in the wind, rain and sun!
For windy days and the chance to fly my kite.
For wet days when I put on my boots and splash about in puddles.
And for sunny days when I run about on the grass in bare feet!
Thank you for looking after me whatever the weather! Amen

Wonderful weather for washing!

There was once a little boat who lived beside a great big lake.

Whenever the sun shone and a gentle breeze blew, she took her friends the fishermen out on the lake to chase fishes!

Her tall masts pointed to the sky… *(point)*

…and her white sails fluttered like washing hung up to dry! *(flap arms)*

But as soon as the noisy wind began to blow…

Whooo…

…and the waves decided to jump and grow…

Splish, splash…

then the little boat came racing back to the beach.

For she was frightened of stormy weather!

As she paddled at the water's edge, the little boat looked out for her friend Jesus. Sometimes he came to sit in the little boat. Then he would tell a story to all the children on the beach.

The little boat listened, too, and she soon forgot all about the big waves in the middle of the lake.

'That *was* a long story,' said Jesus one sunny afternoon. 'I *do* feel tired.

Little boat, will you take me for a sail over to the other side?'

'Yes, yes!' said the little boat, bobbing about with excitement.

'But I hope we don't sail into a storm.'

'Don't worry!' said Jesus. 'I'll be there to look after you.'

The fishermen pushed the little boat out into the smooth, deep water.

The sun shone and a gentle breeze blew.

Flip, flap, whispered the white sails.

Flip, flap!

Slip, slap, murmured the tiny waves.

Slip, slap!

And Jesus fell fast asleep on the warm deck.

All of a sudden, the noisy wind began to blow.

Whooo!

And the waves decided to jump and grow!

Splish, splash!

And the little boat was tossed from side to side.

'Oh dear, oh dear, I'm so frightened!' she cried.

But Jesus kept on sleeping.

'I'll blow a little harder,' roared the wind.

Whooo!

'We'll jump a little higher,' shrieked the waves. 'Look!'

And one jumped so high, that it landed in the little boat with a great big…

CRASH!

But still Jesus kept on sleeping.

'Wake up, Jesus!' shouted the frightened fishermen.

'The waves are jumping into the boat and they're going to push us down to the bottom of the lake.'

'Help, help!'

Then, Jesus *did* wake up.

'Stop it!' he said to the wind.

And the wind stopped blowing.

'Calm down!' he said to the waves.

And the waves grew calm and still.

'Amazing!' said the fishermen.

'Even the wind and the waves obey him!'

The little boat sailed on again under the clear blue sky.

And she spread out her wet sails like washing hung up to dry.

'Isn't this lovely!' she said, with a happy sigh.

'I'm so glad we're sailing with Jesus!'

Craft Sheet

Thank you, God, for fun in the wind, rain and sun! Amen

Cut out another circle of paper the same size as the one on this page. Make two 'peep holes' on opposite sides, large enough for the pictures to be clearly seen through them. Fasten the second circle on top of the weather chart with a split-pin.

JUMP FOR JOY IN THE GARDEN!

Introduction

Encourage the children to use all their senses to appreciate that everything is coming alive in the spring garden, before reading them the wonderful story of Easter. If you make an Easter garden, use it to help tell the story.

Ready...

- Take a seed tray with some soil or wet sand in it, built up into a hill in one corner and covered with moss. Use a few stones to form a cave, with a big stone ready to close the cave.
- Pack the story basket with tiny spring flowers in egg cups, twigs with blossom, furry stems (such as pussy willow) or catkins, a small mirror and some tiny chicks or lambs for the children to put in the Easter garden.
- Have ready a cross made from two twigs.

Steady...

Read: Luke 22:14–23
John 13:1–38
John 16:16–22
John 18:1—20:18

Go...

You're ready to put across the great joy of new life at Easter time.

Let's begin!

Welcome

Welcome everyone! Especially...

Theme

Although Jesus told the disciples that he would rise again on the third day, they did not really understand and thought that his death on the cross was the end of the story. What joy and surprise there was on that first Easter day when their minds finally opened to the truth! When Jesus died on the cross, he conquered death for us. If we really understand the significance of this, what joy there should be in our greeting, 'Happy Easter!'

Notices

Sing Happy Birthday to

The story basket

Say, '*Teddy loves to play in his garden!*' (Bring out the seed tray.) '*He runs about in the grass... and he climbs the hill and rolls down again. But one day in spring, when the sun is shining, Teddy has a big surprise in his garden. He sees some beautiful spring flowers pushing their way up through the grass. Look!*' Bring out the egg cups of flowers and let different children place them in the moss. Point out those that are still tightly shut and those that have opened in the sun.

'*Teddy has another surprise when he looks at the branches of the trees. They are covered in blossom!*' Add the twigs to the garden and let the children feel any furry stems or smell the blossom. Show them the catkins that look like lamb's tails.

'*Teddy's pond sparkles in the sunshine (add the mirror) and he sees fluffy chicks playing (or baby lambs skipping about) in the grass. Everything's coming alive! Teddy is so happy that he jumps for joy in his spring garden.*'

Thank you, God, for all your wonderful spring surprises!

Suggested songs

Mary, Mary, quite contrary
Katie's garden (*Apusskidu*)
A happy time of year (*Feeling Good!*)
Jesus lives again (*Feeling Good!*)
One, two, three, Jesus loves me (*Junior Praise*)

Play-acting

The children curl up in a ball on the floor and pretend to be spring flowers that are still fast asleep under the ground. Spring arrives and they wake up, pushing up through the grass into a standing position and unfurling their arms in the sunshine as if they are petals. (You could hide some chocolate surprises for the children to find in your hall or garden.)

Craft

Fold the page where indicated to hide the chick, and decorate the egg shape on the front. Let the children colour the Easter card.

If you bring some envelopes, the children could hide the cards at home and give someone special a lovely surprise on Easter day.

Prayer

Ask ______________________________ to read today's prayer.

Dear God,
We thank you for all your spring surprises!
For primroses peeping through the grass.
For white blossom on the trees and catkins like lamb's tails.
For fluffy yellow chicks that peck their way out of eggs.
Everything we see is coming alive at Easter time.
Please help us to know that Jesus is alive too.
Amen

Jump for joy in the garden!

Jesus had been working hard, telling everyone about God.

'I must go away soon,' he told his friends. 'But let's have one last supper together.'

That evening, they all met in a special room. Jesus poured some water into a bowl. He began to wash his friends' dusty feet.

'What are you doing, Lord Jesus?' they cried. 'Are you a servant?'

'I am doing this because I love you,' said Jesus. 'And I want you to love one another too!'

Jesus said, 'Love one another!'

They ate bread... *(mime eating)*

...and they drank red wine... *(mime drinking).*

But Judas—who was meant to be a friend—went to fetch some Roman soldiers.

After supper, Jesus and his friends went outside.

They crossed a river into a garden called the Garden of Gethsemane.

The water sparkled in the moonlight and the blossom on the trees made the air smell sweet. It was very late.

'Please stay awake while I pray,' begged Jesus... *(hands together).*

But his friends were too sleepy and they fell asleep... *(heads on hands).*

Then Judas brought the Roman soldiers into the garden.

'Here I am!' said Jesus. The soldiers took Jesus away.

Next morning, the soldiers took Jesus to the palace.

The Roman ruler, called Pilate, said, 'Jesus hasn't done anything wrong!'

'Yes he has!' cried all the people. 'He says he is the Son of God.'

The soldiers put a crown of sharp thorns on Jesus' head. They gave him a heavy wooden cross to carry up the hill... *(place your cross on the hill in the Easter garden).*

They nailed Jesus to the cross and left him there to die.

'Forgive them, Father!' said Jesus. 'They don't know what they are doing.'

The sky went black. The earth shook.

'Now everything is finished!' gasped Jesus, just before he died.

That evening, a kind man called Joseph wrapped Jesus' body in a white sheet. Gently, he laid Jesus in a cave that stood in a beautiful garden. A friend of Jesus, called Mary Magdalene, watched Joseph roll a great big stone in front of the cave to close it... *(close the cave in your garden with the stone).*

Mary went home, feeling sad and lonely.

It is very early on Sunday morning. Mary walks back to the cave. She carries a jar of perfume to pour on the body of Jesus.

'Who will move that big, heavy stone for me?' Mary wonders.

But the cave is already open! The stone is rolled away... *(roll stone).*

Mary hurries to fetch Peter and John. They come running to look in the cave. They see the white sheet lying on the ground.

'The cave is empty!' they cry, full of surprise.

Mary peeps inside the cave. She sees two angels, as white as blossom.

'Don't cry, Mary!' they say, kindly.

Mary turns round and sees a man standing there. She thinks he is the gardener.

'Oh, please, where have you put Jesus?' she asks.

But the man just smiles and says, 'Mary!'

Birds begin to sing. The sun rises and the spring flowers open their petals.

The man isn't the gardener. He is Jesus!

Mary claps her hands... *(clap hands).*

She waves them in the air... *(wave hands).*

'Don't be sad! Be glad!' she tells everybody. 'Jesus is alive!'

Jesus is alive!

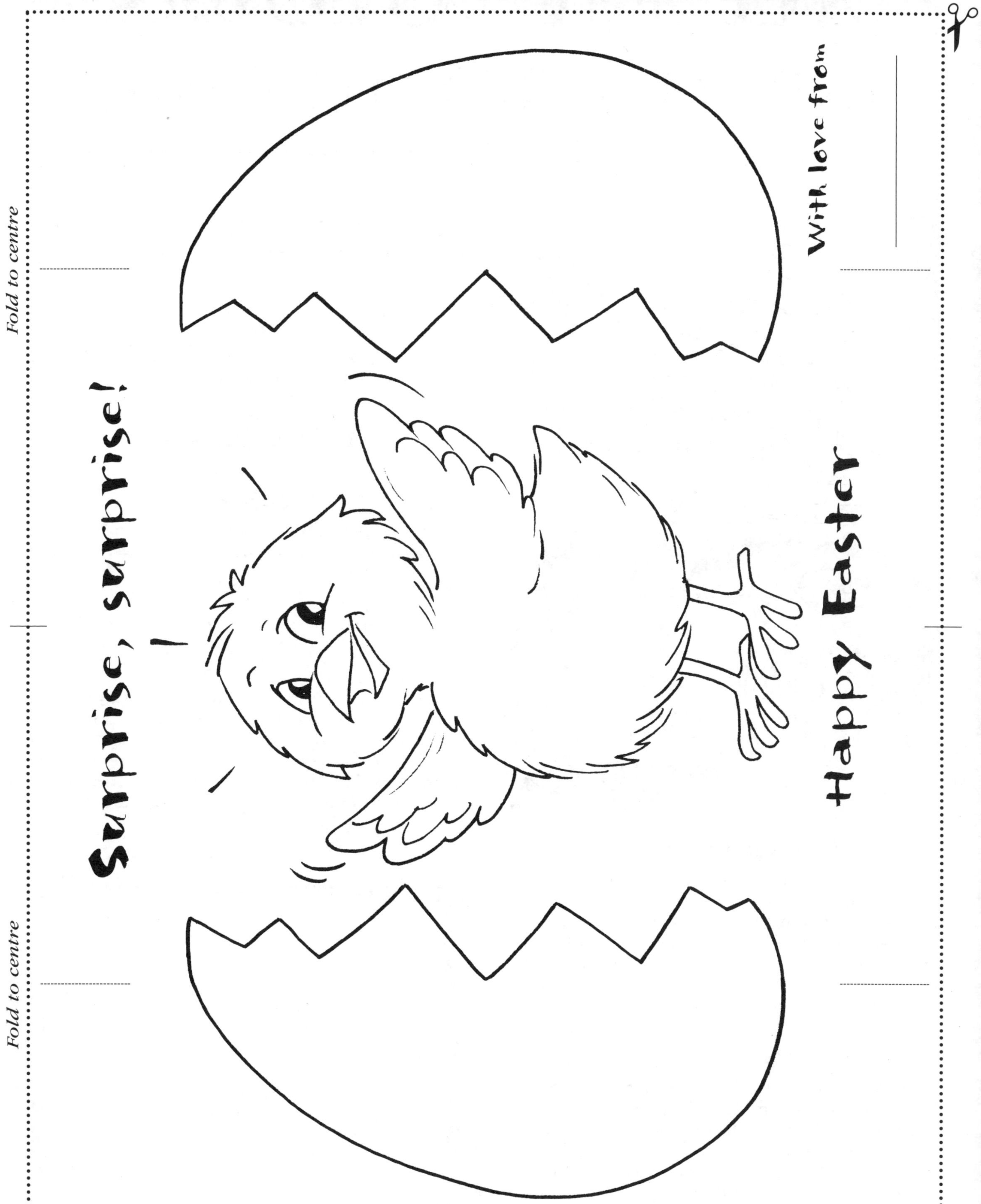

Craft Sheet

Fold to centre

Fold to centre

With love from

Surprise, surprise!

Happy Easter

ALL THE COLOURS OF THE RAINBOW!

Introduction

Use this session to let the children marvel at all the different colours in the world around them, before they listen to the story of Noah's ark. (At harvest time, examine fruit and vegetables that are all colours of the rainbow and thank God for his promise that there will always be a time for planting and a time for harvest.)

Ready...

- Pack the story basket with a child's box of watercolours and some paint brushes, a small pair of wellingtons and a child's umbrella.
- Take along a large sheet of paper (grey, if possible) stuck to a board or tray.
- Or, take different coloured building bricks for the children to sort or build.

Steady...

Read: Genesis 6:9—9:17
1 Peter 5:7

Go...

You're ready to show that we can always trust God to take good care of us.

Let's begin!

Welcome

Welcome everyone! Especially...

Theme

Point out to the adults that rainy days spent indoors with small children can sometimes seem endless. But that stage doesn't last for ever. If we put our trust in God and try to obey his will, we can be sure that he will honour his promise to keep our heads above water!

Notices

Sing Happy Birthday to

The story basket

Explain that Teddy has to stay indoors today because it is going to rain. Say, *'The sky is full of grey clouds. What can Teddy do? Let's see what he can find in the basket!'*

Bring out the paints. *'Hooray! Teddy can paint a beautiful picture!'* Make Teddy paint arcs of different colours on the paper. *'It's a rainbow!'* Explain that a rainbow appears in the sky when the big yellow sun (paint a yellow circle) shines its light through all the raindrops (paint some raindrops).

'Now Teddy wants to go outside and look for a rainbow. But he thinks he might get wet. Don't worry, Teddy. You'll stay dry if you shelter under one of these...' (turn the rainbow into an umbrella by painting a wavy line along the bottom and adding a handle) *'...and if you put on your...'* (paint some red boots).

Teddy finds these items in the basket. He follows the advice and he stays quite dry.

We want to take care of Teddy and God wants to take care of us!

Suggested songs

I hear thunder
Sing a rainbow (*Apusskidu*)
Yellow submarine (*Apusskidu*)
The animals went in two by two (*Apusskidu*)
Colours of the rainbow (*Feeling Good!*)
Mister Noah built an ark (*Junior Praise*)

Play-acting

The children mime pulling on their boots, anoraks and rain-hats. They put up their umbrellas and go for a walk in the rain. They walk through shallow puddles and deep puddles. At the end of the walk, they shake out their umbrellas and tip the water from their boots.

You could teach them the rhyme 'Doctor Foster went to Gloucester in a shower of rain'.

Craft

Help the children to paint or colour the picture. Show older children how to mix colours to make a new colour. What are their favourite colours? What do they like to do on rainy days?

Prayer

Ask ______________________ to read today's prayer.

Dear God,
When the sky turns grey and it starts to rain,
Thank you for your promise that the sun will shine again! **Amen**

All the colours of the rainbow!

'Noah, old friend!' said God one day. 'It's going to rain! It's going to rain and rain and rain... and all the colours of the world will be washed away.'

Noah looked at the beautiful blue sky. It didn't look like rain. But God was always right.

'Will the water come to the top of my boots?' he asked *(touch knees)*.

'Higher!' said God.

'Will it come to the top of my belt?' asked Noah *(touch waists)*.

'Even higher!' said God.

'Will it come to the top of my rain-hat?' asked Noah *(touch heads)*.

'Higher!' said God. 'Even as high as the mountain tops' *(stretch arms up)*.

'Oh, dear,' said Noah. 'Then I'm going to get wet!'

'Noah, old friend,' said God. 'You and your family will stay quite dry. But you must build yourselves a big wooden boat called an ark. Give it a door and lots of rooms and a roof to keep out the rain.'

So Noah began work. He built the boat higher... *(knee high)* and higher... *(waist high)* and higher... *(head high)* until the roof nearly touched the bright blue sky... *(stretch arms up)*

'Now,' said God, 'I want you to fetch animals and birds of every colour and take them into the ark.'

So Noah fetched animals with black, brown and golden fur. And he fetched birds with red, yellow and green feathers.

And he marched them all into the ark, two by two by two.

'Noah, old friend,' said God. 'Take your family into the boat today. It's going to rain soon and everything's going to turn grey.'

So Noah climbed the gangway with Mrs Noah and their boys.

'Rain?' they laughed. 'That sky is blue!'

But Noah knew God's words were true.

'Look,' he said. 'Here comes the first grey cloud.'

'I think I felt rain,' said Mrs Noah. 'Let's go inside.'

Big, fat raindrops fell on to the roof of the boat... *(drum fingers)*.

Then the heavens opened... *(drum faster)* and the boat began to float!

'Well, what did I say?' said Noah. 'All the colours of the world have been washed away!'

'Nothing but rain for forty days!' groaned Mrs Noah. 'I can't get my washing dry.'

'But the wind's getting up,' cried Noah. 'And look! A patch of blue sky!'

The rain stopped. Then slowly, the waters went down... and down... and down... *(mime levels)*.

And the boat came to rest on a mountainside.

'Now,' said Noah, 'who's going to be the first one to step outside?'

There was silence. 'Oh, dear!' said Noah, 'I don't like getting wet.

Let's send a dove to see if there's anything green out there yet.'

The white dove flew in circles and found a twig, all green and dry.

So Noah opened the wooden door, and they saw... a rainbow in the sky!

'Noah, old friend,' said God, 'I've sent this rainbow to say, never again will all the colours of the world be washed away!' Hooray!

After all the rain...
...the sun will shine again!
red
orange
yellow
green
blue
purple

Out and about

ARE WE NEARLY THERE?

Introduction

Use this session to help the children think about long journeys and the various forms of transport, before they listen to the story of Jonah and the whale.

Ready...

- Put into the story basket a few items that Teddy might pack for a long journey and holiday (such as a book, game, swimming-costume, toothbrush and sun-hat) and some toy cars, boats, trains, aeroplanes, as available.
- Take a small suitcase or backpack.

Steady...

Read: Jonah 1:1—3:10
Psalm 139:1–18

Go...

You're ready to explain that wherever we go in the world, we are always within God's care and protection.

Let's begin!

Welcome

Welcome everyone! Especially...

Theme

The thought of a long car journey or flight with young children can often seem daunting. Will they sleep or will they cry endlessly? The story of Jonah and the whale reminds us that however far we travel, God is always with us, helping and caring for us.

Notices

Sing Happy Birthday to

The story basket

Explain that Teddy is looking forward to going away on holiday. He is going to... *(the seaside, the mountains, a big city)*. It will be a long journey to get there. He must pack his bag with all the things that he will need while he is away (bring out the chosen items one by one) and some things to look at on the journey.

Ask different children to pack the items in Teddy's bag. Say, *'I wonder if he'll go on a train'* (bring out the train) *'or on an aeroplane...'* and so on. *'Have you ever been on a long journey?'* Decide how Teddy will travel and ask the children to wave goodbye to him. *'Bye bye! Have a good time, Teddy! Don't forget to read your book on the journey!'*

And if *you* go far away on a long journey, don't forget that God can see you and hear you and he is keeping you safe!

Suggested songs

The wheels on the bus (*Okki-tokki-unga*)
A sailor went to sea, sea, sea (*Okki-tokki-unga*)
Travelling along our lives (*Feeling Good!*)
Wide, wide as the ocean (*Junior Praise*)
If you climb (*Junior Praise*)

Play-acting

Arrange the children's chairs so that they can pretend they are on a bus or an aeroplane, or sit them on a magic carpet! *'Carpet, go to ...... Bye, bye!'*

Travel to different places and mime climbing mountains, swimming in the sea, walking through fields and so on. Older children might suggest places to visit. You might have a naughty carpet that sometimes goes in the wrong direction!

Craft

Cut out the faces and help the children to glue them in the windows of the bus. To make the wheels on the bus 'go round and round', cut out some additional wheels and attach them with paper fasteners. Use the drawing to make a 'Sorry you are leaving' or 'Bon voyage' card.

Prayer

Ask ______________________ to read today's prayer.

Dear God,
How wonderful you are!
When I am playing, you look after me.
When I am asleep, you watch over me.
Wherever I go in the whole wide world,
you keep me safe.
Thank you, God! **Amen**

Are we nearly there?

God spoke to Jonah one day.

'Pack your bags, Jonah! You must travel far away.

Go to the great city of Nineveh.

And tell the people who live there to make friends with me!'

So Jonah packed his bags and he set off... here we go *(walk fingers)*

...in the opposite direction! *(change direction!)*

Oh no!

'That's the wrong way!' cried God. 'Jonah, listen to me!'

But Jonah just kept walking... until he reached the sea.

'I'm not going to Nineveh!' he said. 'God should just be friends with me!'

Jonah saw a ship and he jumped aboard...

...just to get away from the Lord!

'Hee, hee, hee!' laughed Jonah! 'God won't find me!'

Bye, bye! *(wave)*

The sailors pulled up the anchor... *(pull)* and shouted, **'Heave, ho!'**

But Jonah yawned... *(yawn)* and fell fast asleep in the cabin down below.

'Oh, Jonah!' said God sternly. 'Fancy going to sea!

Wherever you go in the world, you cannot hide from me!'

Then God blew upon the water. Waves crashed upon the deck.

The sailors were badly frightened.

'Our ship will be a wreck!'

'God is angry with someone,' they cried, 'but who could it be?'

'Excuse me!' said Jonah, sadly. 'God must be angry with me!

You see, I jumped aboard... just to get away from the Lord!

Now throw me into the sea!'

Bye, bye! *(wave)*

Splash!

Jonah sank down, down to the bottom of the sea.

'Oh, dear,' gurgled Jonah, 'who will rescue me?'

The water ran into his nose.

Waves rolled over his head.

Seaweed stuck to his face.

And he thought he would soon be dead.

Now Jonah was very sorry that he had ever jumped aboard.

And he called out in a frightened voice, 'Can you hear me, Lord?'

'Of course I can hear you,' laughed God. 'I always hear you call.'

Then he sent a big fish to swallow Jonah...

Gulp!

...seaweed and all!

'Bye, bye!' *(wave)*

Bye, bye!

Jonah went slipping and sliding like a mouthful of jelly,

from the fish's big mouth... *(point to mouth)*

...down to the fish's big belly! *(slide finger down to tummy!)*

Then, with Jonah safely inside, the fish swished his tail and took him for a ride!

'What a wonderful God you are!' cried Jonah. 'You heard me pray!

From now on I promise that I'll do what you say!'

So God told the fish to swim towards the land.

And the fish gave a hiccup...

Hic!

...and spat Jonah on to the sand!

'Now, Jonah,' said God. 'To Nineveh, off you go!'

And do you know?

Jonah set off walking... *(walk fingers)* exactly the right way!

Hooray!

Craft Sheet

WHAT'S THE TIME?

Introduction

In this session, the children begin to think about telling the time and the different activities appropriate to each time of day, before listening to the story of Mary and Martha.

Ready...

- Pack the story basket with an attractive children's teaching clock (or use the one from the craft page) and some items to help you tell a story about Teddy's day (see under 'The story basket' below) such as a school tie, a breakfast mug, an exercise book and some crayons, a football, a rubber duck or bath sponge.
- Take some paper fasteners, card or paper plates to make the clock.

Steady...

Read: Luke 10:38–42

Go...

You're ready to encourage the children to find time every day to say their prayers.

Let's begin!

Welcome

Welcome everyone! Especially...

Theme

Parents of young children will know that there is never enough time in the day to do everything! Sometimes it's necessary to do just the important jobs and to leave the rest.

The story of Mary and Martha reminds us that we should never neglect our spiritual lives (prayer, attending church, Bible reading and so on) because we are too busy. If we are steadfast over this, then everything else will fall into place. Encourage parents to create a special time of day when they can pray with their children.

Notices

Sing Happy Birthday to

The story basket

Teddy says, *'What's the time?'* It's time to look in the story basket! Bring out the clock and show the children how the hands move round to tell us the time.

Teddy has a busy day today. *'What does he do at seven o'clock? He gets up and he puts on his school tie... What does he do at eight o'clock? He eats his breakfast and he drinks some milk from his favourite mug...'*

Continue with the story of Teddy's day using examples appropriate to the children in your group. (Use fewer examples for young children.) *'At six o'clock he has a bath and he scrubs behind his ears! Then at seven o'clock he climbs into bed. But wait a minute, Teddy. You've forgotten something very important. What has Teddy forgotten to do? He's forgotten to say his prayers!'*

God loves us and he wants us to talk to him every day. You can speak to him at any time of day because God is always listening!

Suggested songs

Hickory, dickory, dock
Wee Willie Winkie
My grandfather's clock
The best book to read (*Junior Praise*)
Prayer is like a telephone (*Junior Praise*)

Play-acting

Play 'Busy Bees'. Ask the children to move around the room to some music, flapping their elbows and buzzing! When the music stops, they should stand still, ready to mime whatever you say (for example, sweep the floor, read a book, stir the saucepans and so on, and ending with 'say a prayer'!)

Craft

When the children have coloured the clock face, glue it on to a paper plate or card and help them to attach the hands with a paper fastener.

Prayer

Ask ______________________ to read today's prayer.

Dear God,
Thank you for play time and for story time.
Thank you for breakfast time, lunch time and tea time.
Thank you for waking-up time and for bed time.
Thank you that I can talk to you at any time!
Amen

What's the time?

In a little house, in the town of Bethany, there lived two sisters.

Their names both began with an 'M'—Mary and Martha.

But they were as different as could be!

Mary got on with her work very quietly.

And she always found time to stop and watch a cloud floating across the sky... (shield eyes and look up) or to speak to a friend at the well... *(make hands talk)* or just to listen to the birds singing... *(cup ears)*.

But Martha was much too busy for that! She was always sweeping the floor... *(mime sweeping)* or washing the clothes... *(mime scrubbing)* or stirring the food in a pan... *(mime stirring)*.

Everyone said, 'That Martha is as busy as a bee.'

Buzz, buzz, buzz!

'She never stops!'

One day, as Mary gazed out of the window, she saw their friend Jesus coming along the road towards the house.

'Martha!' she cried. 'Here comes Jesus! I wonder if he has any more stories to tell us.'

'Did you say Jesus is coming?' asked Martha. 'Quick, there's no time to lose. Sweep the floor... tidy the clothes... fetch some water, Mary!

I must make him a very special supper.'

Mary went quietly to fetch the water.

But Martha buzzed about the house...

...buzz, buzz, buzz...

...lighting the lamps, and making the fire burn brightly, and chopping up the vegetables and looking out all her pots and pans.

'Where's Martha?' asked Jesus, when he arrived.

'Why, she's busy as usual, cooking the supper,' explained Mary.

'You know Martha! She never stops!'

Jesus washed his hands and his face in the water. Then he sat down and he smiled at Mary.

'Would you like to hear another story?' he asked her.

'It's all about God, my Father, who lives in heaven.'

'Yes, please,' Mary replied.

Martha put another pan over the fire. She could hear Jesus' voice, but the fire crackled so loudly...

...crackle, crackle...

...and the stew bubbled so noisily...

...bubble, bubble...

...that she couldn't quite catch what he was saying.

Martha began to feel cross. It wasn't fair. Why should she do all the work while Mary sat listening to a story?

Martha's face grew hotter and hotter as she bent over the fire.

Crash, bang, wallop...

went the pots and pans, and all of a sudden the stew bubbled right up and splashed over the sides and into the fire.

Then Martha did a very strange thing.

She stopped work and she marched over to where Jesus was sitting.

'Jesus!' she said. 'I'm doing all the work by myself while Mary sits listening to a story. Tell her to come and help me!'

'Oh, Martha, Martha,' said Jesus kindly, taking her hand.

'You are always as busy as a bee.'

Buzz, buzz, buzz!

'Don't worry about cooking me a special supper.

Leave the crackling fire!'

Crackle, crackle!

'Leave the bubbling stew!'

Bubble, bubble!

'Leave all those pots and pans!

Crash, bang, wallop!

'There will be plenty of time for all that tomorrow.

It's much more important to sit down with Mary and listen to my story.'

So that's what Martha did. And everyone said, 'Jesus must be a very special person. Even Martha stops work to listen when he tells a story!'

What's the time?

LOOK OUT OF THE WINDOW!

Introduction

In this session, the children learn to recognize some simple shapes, before listening to the story of creation.

Ready...

- Cut each of the following shapes out of card and put them in the story basket: a yellow circle/sun; a white crescent/moon; yellow or silver stars; green triangles/trees or hills; (if you have time) simple flower, fish, animal and people shapes.
- Take a big piece of rectangular card (perhaps stuck inside a shallow cardboard box) to represent Teddy's window. You could glue tissue paper or material at the sides to look like curtains. Or, put a child's shape sorter with shapes in the basket.
- Take some glitter for the craft page.

Steady...

Read: Genesis 1:1—2:4

Go...

You're ready to inspire the children with wonder at the beauty and diversity of the world they can see out of the window.

Let's begin!

Welcome

Welcome everyone! Especially...

Theme

Point out to any adults present that in having children we are taking part in the story of creation. The Bible story reminds us of the power of words. ('Let there be light'—and there was light.) We may not be able to create something from nothing, as God can, but we can use words to praise all that is good about our children and so encourage them to flourish.

Notices

Sing Happy Birthday to

The story basket

Tell the children that Teddy is learning his shapes. Perhaps they could help him. One by one, bring out the circle, triangle, crescent (a smiley shape) and star shapes from the basket for the children to identify. Praise their efforts! (Older children could draw the shapes in the air.)

Explain that God's world is full of wonderful shapes.

Teddy wants to look out of his window to find out how many shapes he can see. Ask the children to help you make a beautiful

view for Teddy on the card using all the different shapes. (See the craft page for some ideas.) Say, '*Which shape shall we use for the sun? The circle, that's right, Emily. Would you like to come and put it in the sky for Teddy? Who made the sun? God did!*' ... and so on. Teddy is delighted with the view from his window (he claps his paws).

Thank you, God, for our wonderful world!

Suggested songs

Round and round the garden
My hat it has three corners (*Okki-tokki-unga*)
Clap! Clap! What a wonderful world (*Feeling Good!*)
All things bright and beautiful (*Junior Praise*)
Who put the colours in the rainbow? (*Junior Praise*)

Play-acting

Ask the children to close their eyes and to imagine that they are sitting in the most beautiful garden they have ever seen. Can they picture the trees, the flowers, the butterflies? Look at all the different shapes!

Now they open their eyes and walk around the room with an imaginary basket. Prompt them to mime picking a flower, plucking an apple, chasing a butterfly and so on, and finish by lying down and gazing at the stars.

Craft

Ask the children what they can see out of their own window at home as they decorate the picture. What are their favourite shapes?

Or, cut out shapes from the natural world (such as a tree or a ladybird) and let them colour and stick on, for example, round apples or spots (as appropriate).

Make a creation collage and put it together as you read the story.

(To link in with St Valentine's Day, ask the children to stick small pieces of crumpled red tissue paper on a heart shape.)

Prayer

Ask ______________________________ to read today's prayer.

Thank you, God, for all the lovely shapes we can see, out of the window.
Thank you for birds in the air,
and fruit on the tree.
Thank you for animals in the fields,
and fish in the sea!
Thank you, God, for making me! **Amen**

Look out of the window!

Look out of your window! What can you see?
  Children, clouds, a flower—a hill, a bird, a tree!
  But where did everything come from? How did the world begin?
  Listen to the story of creation which begins with God!

In the beginning, God looked out at nothing!
  There was nothing for God to see.
  No shapes, no shadows, no colours—just darkness and a swirling sea.
  So God closed his eyes and looked instead,
  at all the beautiful shapes that shone inside his head:
  spinning circles… crescents… and stars that danced with light… *(draw or hold up these shapes in the air)*
  He would SAY each word and make the darkness bright!

'Let there be light!' said God.
  His words floated in the darkness, almost lost.
  Then, in a flash, they sparkled like frost!
  'How beautiful!' said God, his eyes twinkling in the light.
  'I will call this brightness "day". And the darkness I'll call "night".'

God looked all around him, near and far.
  But he couldn't see a home for all his circles… crescents… and stars…
  'Let there be a great dome,' he cried. 'Wide and high!'
  Then up flew his words in an archway… *(arch arms above heads)*
  …and made the sky!

'And while I think of it,' he said, 'Let there be dry land!'
  So the waters ran to meet the sea and God stood on the sand!

'Now,' said God, pleased. 'I've made the land, the sky, and sea.
But everything is empty. There are *still* no shapes to see!'

He looked down at the dull, brown earth where nothing grew.
And he sprinkled it with words and watered them with dew.
'Let there be flowers with oval petals that nod their heads in the breeze!
Let rounded apples and oranges hang from leafy triangular trees!'
Then tiny pointed shoots pushed through the earth in every place.
And a smile, the shape of a banana, grew upon God's face!
(Draw smiley shape on faces!)

'It's time to fill the sky!' he cried at last.
And in this lofty space, he found just the place
to hang each circle... crescent... and star...
And very soon, the day was lit by sunshine...
and the night time by the moon!

God looked at the sea and the empty waves.
And he longed for shapes that dived and splashed and hid in rocky caves.

'Let there be star-fish and angel-fish and whales as big as a tree!'
Then his words grew scales and fins and tails...
and swam right out to sea!

He looked at the sky and out flew these words:
'Let the air be filled with different shaped birds.'
And he looked at the land with its great empty plots:
'Let there be creatures with different shaped spots!'

Then God saw his own reflection in the water.
And he said, 'Let me make myself a son and a daughter!'

God gazed at the world he had shaped from the start.
And he blew it a kiss in the shape of... A HEART!!

Look out of the window!
red
glitter
yellow
green

FURTHER IDEAS

Suggestions for speakers

You may like to invite speakers along from time to time to talk to the adults as they have their coffee. If the children will be in the same room, it's probably best to keep the talks to ten minutes. Ask local speakers who won't mind popping in for such a short time (or someone who already belongs to the group). They will enjoy joining you for a coffee and a chat and a chance to get to know the children. Try to link the theme with your topic. Here are a few suggestions for some of the sessions.

One, two, three... God made me

Ask a local portrait painter or sculptor to talk about their work. Ask a photographer to take pictures of the children.

I'm only small...

Ask the expert at your local children's shoe shop to talk on 'Your child's first pair of shoes' or 'Shoes for growing feet'.

I don't feel very well!

'When to call the doctor' or 'The pre-school check-up'.

With love from me to you

'Make your own Christmas cards' or 'Gift wrapping for Christmas'.

Jump for joy in the garden!

'Make an Easter flower arrangement (or table decoration).'

Are we nearly there?

'Tips on travelling with young children.'

What's the time?

A display of prayer books and Bible story books for children from the local Christian bookshop.

Pram service

You could hold a short pram service in your church at Christmas and Easter and invite everyone back to the hall afterwards for coffee and mince pies or hot cross buns. Use the ideas from this book as a starting point. For example, a simple Easter service sheet based on *Jump for joy in the garden!* on pages 61–67 might be:

(Give the group's name)

Easter Pram service

(Date)

(You could choose a Bible verse from the Ready, Steady, Go! section and print it out here.)

⁕

Welcome and introduction

(Adapt the 'Theme' paragraph as necessary, perhaps saying that all the signs of new life in the garden remind us that Jesus conquered death on the cross and that he is alive.)

⁕

Hymn or song

⁕

The children help to assemble a miniature spring garden

⁕

Hymn or song

⁕

The Easter story

(Briefly tell the story, adding the cross to the garden and rolling the stone to close and then open the cave.)

⁕

Hymn or song

⁕

Prayer

⁕

Blessing

HAPPY EASTER EVERYONE!

Please join us in the hall afterwards for coffee and hot cross buns!

You could hold a summer service, too, followed by a teddy bear's picnic.